Ivy Compton-Burnett

by BLAKE NEVIUS

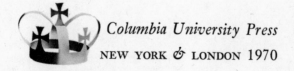

Columbia University Press

NEW YORK *&* LONDON 1970

COLUMBIA ESSAYS ON MODERN WRITERS is a series of critical studies of English, Continental, and other writers whose works are of contemporary artistic and intellectual significance.

Editor: William York Tindall

Advisory Editors

Jacques Barzun   W. T. H. Jackson   Joseph A. Mazzeo

Ivy Compton-Burnett is Number 47 of the series

BLAKE NEVIUS is Professor of English at the University of California, Los Angeles. He is the author of *Edith Wharton: A Study of Her Fiction* and *Robert Herrick: The Development of a Novelist.*

Copyright © 1970 Columbia University Press
SBN: 231–02988–8
Library of Congress Catalog Card Number: 74–110600
Printed in the United States of America

6461

Ivy Compton-Burnett

The day may never come when Ivy Compton-Burnett has the audience in the United States that she deserves. Her work has been intermittently sponsored by American publishers, first in the early thirties and much later (after an interval in which publication of her work was evidently a casualty of the depression) following the success of *Bullivant and the Lambs* in 1947. There have been consequent small flurries of critical interest succeeded by periods of neglect. Though in England her reputation is formidable and secure and the debate is merely over whether she is a major novelist or not quite a major novelist, in this country her novels either excite zealous partisanship or are dismissed, somewhat thoughtlessly, as arid, repetitive, and willfully eccentric. There is, it would seem, no temperate zone of response. Only one of the book-length critical studies of her fiction has been published here, and almost none of the better critical articles.

The situation is all the odder because she is not only one of the most interesting and original novelists of our century but one of the most relevant. Her novels, written during the cataclysmic years between 1925 and 1963, provide an obliquely penetrating commentary on the nature and abuses of power. Though their conflicts are limited to the domestic arena and though with one exception their actions occur between 1885 and 1902, the internecine struggle which defines her world takes place in a timeless present. "The miniature world of the family!" exclaims one of her characters. "All the emotions of mankind seem to find a place in it." Miniature and self-contained it may be, but its people and events extend their meanings irresistibly into the larger world; and though in one sense it may have faded into the Victorian twilight, it offers no refuge from the persecuted present. Ironically, however, what for our time should be the most salutary trait of her novels, their astringent moral quality, probably has helped limit their appeal quite as much as their close texture, their stylization, and their determined intellectuality.

Her first novel, *Dolores* (which in later years she described as "juvenilia" and tried to disown), is a failure. But like so many first novels it is interesting simply because it is less circumspect than its successors. Though it is doubtful that anyone knows finally how to take it, *Dolores*, published in 1911 when Miss Compton-Burnett was in her late twenties, gives the impression of a deeply personal work. Its tone is mainly sentimental, sometimes lugubrious, but at other times faintly ironic, as if the author had set out to write the ultimate Victorian novel, in a state of mind at once pious and irreverent, and without intending to, produced an uncertain parody. She owes a great deal, as some critics have noted, to the great nineteenth-century novelists of her own sex, Jane Austen, the Brontës, Mrs. Gaskell, and George Eliot, though she seems to have espoused them in a solemnly feminist mood. Her plot, for one thing, takes its cue from the most familiar theme in their fiction, the claims of passion versus those of duty. If the reader heeds the logic of event he will conclude that the author of *Dolores* is opting for passion, but if he succumbs to the earnest schoolgirl tone that informs most of the novel he will be inclined to take seriously the frequent paeans to duty and self-sacrifice and accept *Dolores* as an anachronism difficult to comprehend in the era of Shaw, Forster, and Samuel Butler.

[4]

Dolores must be one of the most long-suffering and uncompensated heroines in fiction. The plain eldest daughter of the Reverend Cleveland Hutton, a widower of no means, she devotes her best years to managing the domestic concerns of a father who obviously needs her less than she thinks he does, for he marries twice after the death of Dolores's mother, fathers a second batch of children, and discovers in his third marriage a conjugality so rewarding that Dolores is finally and irrevocably displaced from the family circle. At seventeen she enters a girls' college on a scholarship to prepare herself for a teaching career. There she meets and falls in love with Sigismund Claverhouse, fiftyish, solitary, poor, and physically grotesque, who commutes from Oxford and the house he shares with his devoted octogenarian mother to teach at Dolores's school. He also writes unplayable dramas, presumably in the manner of Ibsen. Dolores becomes his worshiping disciple, perfectly willing to play Dorothea to his Casaubon except that she owes her first duty to her father, who summons her home at strategic intervals to solve the domestic crises. Claverhouse's mother dies. In his desolation he falls in love with Dolores's school friend Perdita (her name, like that of Dolores, prophetic of her fortune) and proposes. Perdita, on the rebound from an unhappy passion for Dolores's ineffectual brother Bertram, accepts him. Nine months later she dies in childbirth, and Claverhouse reads in her diary the despairing chronicle of her life with him. He turns to Dolores for comfort, but she is called home by the death of her stepmother. Five years pass before she sees him again, now blind, petulant, and hopeless, and is able to resume her devotions at the flickering shrine. When Claverhouse dies she returns again to the parsonage. But her father has married again. Dolores has no place, no function, no prospects. Eventually she is persuaded to return to the college. At thirty-three, irredeemably plain and finally alone, she has tea with her spinster colleagues, listens to their chatter, and knows that this is the shape of her future.

On the evidence of such a Griselda-like saga, it would appear that the young Ivy Compton-Burnett is entering her protest against the hard lot of women in a society devised for the comfort of men. It is not that simple, however. The only young man on the scene is the invertebrate Bertram, who foreshadows all those parent-ridden, incompetent young men of the later novels, as Dolores does that long succession of victimized governesses. The dominant male figures are older men, well advanced into middle age—the Reverend Mr. Hutton, Claverhouse, and the latter's bachelor friend Soulsby—and it is they and their contemporaries with whom not only Dolores but her friend Perdita and her half-sister Sophia fall in love or marry. Rejected by the father, they seek the father surrogate. This unrewarded devotion of daughter to father is one of the commonest motifs in the later novels; so is the callous and self-regarding behavior of the fathers in relation to their children; and so is the tendency of Miss Compton-Burnett's young women to marry much older men, for reasons of expedience if not of passion. It is tempting, in fact, to see a figure in the carpet in this cluster of motifs, and as woven into it that other most familiar and intense familial relationship, the one between brother and sister, which appears in every novel. The Dolores-Claverhouse relationship may owe something to *Middlemarch* and to *Jane Eyre* (which, as Kathleen Tillotson observes, "started the vogue for plain heroines and ugly masterful heroes"), but it goes through so many permutations in the later novels that it is difficult not to view it as a psychic pattern which evolved independently of literary precedents.

It is dangerous to carry the game further. Regarding her personal life, Miss Compton-Burnett was the most reticent novelist of her time. "Autobiography is not my line," she insisted, "and my life has to the outside eye been uneventful." Her childhood, a friend has written, is "largely irrecoverable," for she had taken care to cover her tracks. Born in Pinner, Middlesex, on June 5, 1884 (until her death the year was given as 1892), the eldest child of her father's second marriage, she grew up mainly in Hove and Richmond, in one of those large Victorian families she anatomizes in her fiction. Her father, James Compton-Burnett, was a doctor, who died when Ivy was sixteen. Her mother was, like the mothers in so many of her novels, remote. "She loved us," her daughter admitted, "but she didn't like us very much." Like the children in her novels, who marshal themselves into phalanxes determined by their age groups, Ivy and her two younger brothers, to whom she was devoted, formed a defensive unit within the family. Educated in her early years at home, in the nursery and schoolroom which figure so largely in her fictional setting, she later took a degree in Classics at Royal Holloway College of the University of London. The early deaths of her brothers—one died of pneumonia, the other was killed in the Battle of the Somme—contributed to the serious illness which helps explain the fourteen-year silence between the publication of *Dolores* and of *Pastors and Masters* (1925). For over thirty years, Miss Compton-Burnett shared a London flat with her friend Margaret Jourdain, an authority on antique furniture, who died in 1951. Besides writing, her chief enthusiasms seem to have been the London theater and botanizing in the Swiss Alps. An agnostic, she claims to have shed her belief in Christianity around the age of ten.

Nothing much here to explain the sudden reemergence in *Pastors and Masters* of a dormant talent or the startling unconventionality of its expression. *Pastors and Masters* is the merest sketch of a novel, as its equivocal subtitle "A Study" may suggest, but it introduces a new manner, a new idiom, and an angle of vision as remote from that of *Dolores* as it is from that of most of Miss Compton-Burnett's novel-writing contemporaries. When Emily Herrick, the ostensible protagonist of the story, remarks that "the sight of duty does make one shiver," we know that the lurking anti-thesis of *Dolores* has surfaced. From now on the hypocrisies practiced by the elders and the penalties exacted from the young in the name of duty will be dealt with unambiguously. Though the plot of *Pastors and Masters* is designed mainly to accommodate the talk, it is at once too simple and too elaborate. Its main element is a double fraud involving a manuscript, and the burden this imposes on the plot is tolerable only because it helps reflect the general corruption in the microcosm of a provincial boarding school.

Miss Compton-Burnett's audience for this cheerfully sinister novella were few but hardly fit. With one or two exceptions, the critics who read it dismissed it as merely odd. After all, what was one to say of a work of fiction that dispensed with almost every means thought useful or appropriate to fiction, whose action was presented almost entirely through dialogue and sustained not by exposition and narrative but by a kind of intermittent gloss that reminded one of stage directions—a work that starved the visual imagination but demanded an alert ear and an unflagging attention? Here was the novel *démeublé* with a vengeance. The plot appeared to be improvised and uncoordinated, the transitions from one phase of the action to the next were barely indicated, and the setting was vague—a third-rate school, location unspecified, in the years following World War I. To its earliest audience the whole thing must have had the air of a private joke, which would have been enhanced by the cryptic signature "I. Compton-Burnett" making the sex of the author as indeterminate as that of some of the characters.

As for the dialogue which would prove to be the hallmark of Miss Compton-Burnett's method: already it had its own

[8]

cadences and inflections; it was brittle, arch, emphatic. But it was distinctive mainly because the characters had no reserves, or appeared to have none. They had not the habit, as a character in one of the later novels puts it, of "editing" themselves. In the most literal sense they seemed to be speaking their minds, obeying every fugitive impulse toward self-expression, and by this means implying that they had no concealed depths, no private life, no secrets. At the same time, it was part of their dilemma that though they communicated freely they were invariably misunderstood. However, by the time one of the characters in *Pastors and Masters* remarks, in the last chapter, "How good we all are at talking without saying what we think," the reader has been made sufficiently aware of the network of hypocrisy binding this provincial academic society together that he is not likely again to accept as invariably honest coin the self-revelations of Miss Compton-Burnett's characters. It is one of the difficult problems posed at the outset by Miss Compton-Burnett's method, to determine when her characters are revealing, when disguising themselves; for although they unburden themselves with apparent candor, they are apt to conceal their deepest motives. It is a problem intensified of course by the novelist's detachment, her refusal except on rare and necessary occasions to penetrate her characters' minds directly or to analyze, except through conventional dramatic means, their hidden or unconscious motives.

Pastors and Masters is a Compton-Burnett novel in embryo. The full authority of the novelist's gifts is realized for the first time in *Brothers and Sisters*, published four years later. One of Miss Compton-Burnett's half-dozen finest novels, it represents an enormous gain in wit and humanity over her prentice work. It was reviewed widely, and in some quarters with bafflement or outrage, but the years have enhanced its stature. The plot is as complicated—and at first glance as apparently sportive—as any

[9]

Miss Compton-Burnett invented. It involves what are to become the standard ingredients—incest, illegitimacy, the domestic inquisition, the family secret which becomes public knowledge, and a spectrum of vices ranging from eavesdropping to will-burning. Sophia Stace, the daughter of octogenarian Andrew Stace, marries in defiance of the latter's injunction her adopted brother Christian. Twenty-five years later, after they have raised three children now in their early twenties, Sophia and her husband discover that Christian is the illegitimate son of Andrew, that they are consequently half brother and sister, and that their children are the offspring of an incestuous union. From its inception the tragedy has been the product of Sophia's overriding will. It is she who takes the initiative in defying her father, who suppresses the old man's will disinheriting his children if they marry, and who inadvertently brings to light her father's letter revealing her true relation to Christian. The revelation is followed by Christian's fatal heart attack and Sophia's collapse. Matriarchal to the end, Sophia continues to exert the tyranny of her will through invalidism, and ultimately dies of cancer. But in this reenactment of the Fall it is the children who suffer most deeply, for they must go on living with the guilt, the isolation, and the despair.

If none of this sounds complicated, but merely melodramatic, it should be added that including Christian and Sophia there are six pairs of brothers and sisters in the cast and that among them are the children of Christian's mother, who, sharing the general ignorance, are about to become engaged to Andrew and Dinah Stace. The plot has in fact ramifications which can only be suggested, with the assurance that Miss Compton-Burnett exploits to their limit the incestuous entanglements.

Given such a plot, one of the questions that poses itself on the threshold of any discussion of Miss Compton-Burnett's method is that of her intended tone, a question that involves the varying and often confusing degrees of seriousness which inform her manner as opposed to her themes. Among her critics there seems to be no consensus on the answer nor, presumably, any real sense of its urgency, and this may be the only practical wisdom in dealing with a novelist who insisted that tragedy and comedy are inseparable in fiction and who, in her own words, "shouldn't mind being described as amoral" because she had an equal affection for her good and bad characters and worked on the premise "that crime on the whole pays." It is tempting, moreover, to accept at face value Miss Compton-Burnett's frequent but always unexpected assertions of the value of a strong plot. "It seems to me that a book must have a structure," she once remarked. "It may be an old-fashioned view, but I am surprised by some of these modern books, which have no structure at all." In practice, however, she gives the impression of being not quite serious about her plots, and it is equally tempting to see in this attitude merely a reflection of those other idiosyncrasies such as borrowing her titles from the stock of minor Victorian fiction, naming her characters after the great and not-so-great writers in the history of English literature, and exploiting unashamedly such melodramatic devices as lost earrings, suppressed wills, overheard conversations, and concealed identities. The structure of her plots is always prominent but at the same time disproportionate; it follows no customary curve of development. Individual scenes are often unreasonably attenuated. And yet it is in the individual scenes that Miss Compton-Burnett's sense of drama is most acute. When as happens occasionally the polite surface is shattered, we have episodes of remarkable intensity, such as the passage-at-arms between Harriet Haslam and her oldest son in *Men and Wives* or the dinner-table scene in *Daughters and Sons* in which Hetta Ponsonby turns on her family and denounces them. But these moments are not always placed so that they tell in relation to the action as a

6461

whole; their effectiveness depends simply on their violation of the usual atmosphere of constraint in which the conflict is waged.

However, taking the conventional view of Miss Compton-Burnett's plots and making the conventional objections only points up the fact that any criticism of her fiction must begin and end with a consideration of the deliberate limitations she imposes on her material and treatment. One of the most obvious is the restricted setting of her novels. In her earliest public statement Miss Compton-Burnett admitted her temperamental inability to find herself in the present: "I do not feel that I have any real or organic knowledge of life later than about 1910. I should not write of later times with enough grasp or confidence." Since her one subject is the family, she might have added that the late nineteenth century became her special province because the family then was more closely bound together, its younger members more pliant to authority and therefore more demonstrably at the mercy of tyranny exercised from above. Moreover, if her style is any clue we can be certain that her imagination was possessed completely by the world of her girlhood, for it has all the characteristics that Bonamy Dobrée finds in the style deriving from that essentially ordered and complacent period before World War I: it is formal and emphatic; each sentence contains an idea and completes it, so that we have no reflection of the headlong uninterrupted flow of thought or of the felt immediacy of experience. "In the Twentieth Century you feel like movement," wrote Gertrude Stein. "The Nineteenth Century didn't feel that way." Unlike the equally personal styles of Miss Stein, Virginia Woolf, or Hemingway, Miss Compton-Burnett's style betrays none of the tensions or uncertainties of modern life, and it appears untroubled by an awareness of the subconscious.

[12]

Physically, Miss Compton-Burnett's world is bounded by the walls of the country house and, in three novels at least, the public school. Though the scene may be broadened occasionally to include the village shop, the rectory lawn, or the neighbor's parlor, the locomotive impulse of her characters, like the range of their interests, is so severely limited that a walk in the park unexpectedly enlarges our horizon. It is this confinement to the narrow provincial sphere, and the capacity at the same time to transcend it, that has led so many critics to couple Miss Compton-Burnett's name with that of Jane Austen—the Jane Austen who remarked that "three or four families in a country village is the thing to work on"—before it was conceded that the comparison, like so many to which Miss Compton-Burnett has been subjected, is not very helpful and on the whole misleading.

In the novels as a group the economic and social factors remain constant. We have the author's word for it that some of her characters work for a living, as lawyers, doctors, novelists, government clerks, small shopkeepers, but their vocations—unless they are employed in the household as tutors, governesses, or servants—are never obtrusive. Her little world is hermetically sealed off from the contamination of business and politics, though emphatically not, as this might imply, from the influence of money. Through the pages of *The Times* its inhabitants may preserve a tenuous connection with the great world of science and art and progress, but for the most part they cherish their isolation. Almost all of the families in the novels are financially embarrassed. The country squires support their large families and host of dependents precariously on the diminishing income from rents and dowries. For better or worse—and invariably it is the latter—economic pressure welds the family together. The mutual antagonisms within its circle are held in check by the instinct of self-preservation, so that we have the

[13]

spectacle of dependent elder brothers, younger brothers, widowed sisters, cousins, unfitted for the work of the world, encouraging against their will the free play of tyranny.

The world of Miss Compton-Burnett has its own peculiar ecology. In this domestic arena where the life-and-death struggle takes place, the combatants are unevenly matched. "We all have a right to survive," says Hope Cranmer (*Parents and Children*), "and only the fittest can do so, and it seems that a struggle is inevitable." Life feeds on life, within a precarious system of physical and psychological adaptation. Abovestairs, in the nursery and schoolroom, the older children victimize the younger and both make life hell for the tutors and governesses; belowstairs, butler and cook exercise their tyranny over footman and maid; and the hierarchy is topped by their elders and betters who, consciously or unconsciously, are leagued against the younger and weaker. Where this balance is disturbed, blighted areas appear and spread and are contained only when the antagonists strike a new balance at a less satisfactory level. In the meantime, in proving their fitness to survive, Miss Compton-Burnett's characters have no great regard for the decalogue. Their mildest transgressions are eavesdropping and opening other people's mail; on more stringent occasions they are equal to theft, murder, forgery, and adultery. "How wicked everyone is!" exclaims Mortimer Lamb (*Bullivant and the Lambs*). "There does not seem to be a single exception." There *are* exceptions—Mortimer is one of them—and their goodness, as Henry Reed says, "glows like a distant sun through a frosted window." But they are mostly ineffectual. They wither and die, or like Mortimer are subtly corrupted. And they share the fate of other good people in literature in that they impose themselves much less vigorously on the reader's imagination than do the characters whose will to power invests their roles with a terrifying significance.

[14]

Beginning with the Reverend Mr. Bentley in *Pastors and Masters* and extending through Ninian Middleton in *The Mighty and Their Fall* (1961), Miss Compton-Burnett created a memorable gallery of tyrants. Their power is conferred by money, position, character, invalidism, or by a formidable combination of these advantages, and it is reinforced by a consuming egoism. Their collective slogan is formulated by Duncan Edgeworth (*A House and Its Head*): "I have been a rule to myself." They find the meaning of their existence only in the visible waste they are able to produce in the destinies under their control—especially those of their children, since to destroy what one has created is the ultimate satisfaction of the will to power. In the most literal sense this is what Miss Compton-Burnett's tyrants accomplish by the destructive force of their personalities: the early blighting of the lives of their children, whom they treat callously or at best with blundering incomprehension.

Because Miss Compton-Burnett's victims exhibit the progressive attrition of will that accompanies dependence on a stronger will, the aftermath of tyranny in her stories is frightening in the same way and for the same reasons that it is in a country that has suffered total military defeat—as, for example, in post-Hitler Germany. When the tyrant dies, the sudden removal of authority creates a tragic void in which the victims flounder hopelessly. Mere anarchy is loosed upon the small domestic world. Similarly, if power is only temporarily in abeyance, because the tyrant falls ill or takes a trip or is unaccountably struck with remorse, there is an unhappy interval until it reasserts itself, during which the victims realize their inadequacy and accept their fate.

At first glance, Miss Compton-Burnett seems to be as limited in her range of characterization as in her themes and setting. Her characters tend to marshal themselves into a few general categories: parents, children, relatives, servants, neighbors, and the pathetic host of tutors, masters, governesses, and schoolmistresses. Within these categories certain types reappear regularly: the effete young men, fond of the society of old ladies; the plain-speaking middle-aged spinsters; the incompetent husbands and fathers (when the family organization is matriarchal) and the gentle, ailing wives (when it is patriarchal); the old men preoccupied with the fact of their mortality, envious of the young, the dignity of whose years is being constantly marred by the unexpected appearance of their illegitimate children; the drab governesses who are supporting their parents; the inquisitive neighbors, who function like a Greek chorus, commenting, warning, lamenting (but who disappear from the later novels with their narrower focus and progressive economy of means); and the butlers, who are discreet in the dining room, indiscreet in the kitchen. What is apt to strike the reader most sharply is the way Miss Compton-Burnett confounds the usual distinctions: her old men are frequently childish, her children wise beyond their years, her young men old. The novels are full, moreover, of masculine women and feminine men, individuals for the most part undifferentiated as to sex. "What I have noticed," says Josephine Napier (*More Men Than Women*), ". . . is that in highly developed people the mental force is often out of scale with the physical." These *are* highly developed people, and because on the intellectual level the distinction of sex is apt to be blurred, there is a lack of passional emphasis in the relations between the sexes. People in Miss Compton-Burnett's novels marry, but one wonders how they manage to produce their large families, because their creator is primarily interested in the relations between brother and sister, father and daughter, mother and son. As Thomas Calderon (*Elders and Betters*) remarks of his wife's family: "The brothers and sisters are so bound up in each other that even their children seem

[16]

apart. They should have been able to reproduce like some lower forms of life by means of pieces broken off themselves." It is difficult, as a matter of fact, to avoid the suspicion that they do.

But the generalization that her characters run to types has obscured the fact—possibly overemphasized by some of her admirers—that Miss Compton-Burnett conceived a large number of highly individualized characters. They are not "memorable," for the same reasons that, as E. M. Forster complains, Virginia Woolf's characters are not memorable. They do not lodge themselves in the reader's mind by the force of their visual reality, by the cumulative impression of appearance, manners, tone of voice, habits, gestures. Miss Compton-Burnett may have been influenced by the progressive deemphasis on objective aids to characterization initiated by such novelists as Mrs. Woolf and D. H. Lawrence. Her characters, like theirs, are defined primarily through their relationships; they emerge through a very complicated interaction between personalities and motives. Consequently, for many readers they lack individuality, though in what appears to be a polite or mock concession to those readers Miss Compton-Burnett introduces them with a quaint formality. In the earlier novels her packaged descriptions managed, usually by the inclusion of a single sharp detail, to convey the impression of individuality. Emily Herrick (*Pastors and Masters*) has "a face that somehow recalled an attractive idol's"; Richard Bumpus, in the same novel, is "a little dark man about fifty-six, with eyes sunk deeply in a working face." In the novels of her middle period the descriptions become more generalized, begin to conform to the character types by now so well established. They lean heavily on manner: the opposition, balancing, or calculated repetition of certain adjectives. Her composite character is prominently fair or dark, has a figure solid or lean, features narrow or broad, and wears an absent or alert expression.

[17]

Although the visual reality of her characters is blurred and ultimately lost as the action unfolds, there is a constant gain in the clarity of their relationships. They manage to survive in the reader's memory, not solidly fleshed and possessing a life apart from that of the other characters, as do Becky Sharp and Mr. Pickwick, but in the context of particular situations, as factors in a variable problem of familial relationships. We may visualize them as we please. "I am sure," their creator once said, "that everyone forms his own conceptions, that are different from anyone else's, including the author's."

Miss Compton-Burnett's children deserve special mention. She does not sentimentalize them. She is capable of remarking of the Clare children's relation to their nurse (*The Past and the Present*), "They loved her not as themselves, but as the person who served their love of themselves, and greater love has no child than this." But beginning in the forties they figure with increasing importance in the novels and acquire a pathetic stature that earlier was missing. In *Pastors and Masters* they exist—some forty small boys—in the background as the nameless, faceless victims of the group of eccentric adults who are responsible for their mental, physical, and spiritual growth; but in the next six novels the "children" are in their late teens or twenties. No more capable than their juniors of resisting tyranny, they have at least the cushioning advantage of their years and the compensation of being able to inflict cruelty on those younger and weaker than themselves. Beginning with *Parents and Children* (1941), however, it is the younger children who are the prime candidates for martyrdom.

Miss Compton-Burnett treats with special tenderness the dilemma of her children who are not young enough to be unaware of what is happening to them and not old enough to have acquired protective armor, those who have reached the in-between age of from ten to fourteen (for example, James Sullivan in *Parents and Children*, Reuben Donne in *Elders and Betters*, Clemence and Sefton Shelley in *Two Worlds and Their Ways*). The pattern of their destiny never varies. From an early age they are burdened with an intolerable sense of their dependency. They are made to feel guiltily responsible for the unhappiness of their parents, and they are called on regularly to furnish testimonials of their gratitude, familial piety, and love. Forced beyond the limit of their natural abilities to excel in school, they learn to cheat, lie, and evade. When the tissue of deceit that envelops their family life is exposed, they are compelled to participate fully with their elders in the revelation, and the result is a sudden, enforced maturity which destroys the few illusions they have managed to retain. Their wills crippled and their sensibilities hardened by the mutually reinforcing influences of home and school, they grow into adulthood conforming to the image of their oppressors. Tyranny perpetuates itself. "This harsh upbringing will make hard women of us all," observes one of the schoolgirls in *Two Worlds and Their Ways*. "We shall want other people to suffer as we have." Meanwhile, these present victims may read their future as it is projected in the careers of their older brothers and sisters, who languish at home in uneasy thralldom or, when circumstances permit, testify to the grim efficacy of their training by becoming tyrants themselves. From generation to generation the cycle of oppression is renewed. "We grow to the life we lead," says John Ponsonby, in *Daughters and Sons*. "We are moulded to it and by it. It becomes our own."

One final matter before returning to the individual novels. Margaret Jourdain, in her 1945 conversation with Miss Compton-Burnett, called her friend's novels "conversation pieces stepping into the bounds of drama," and Miss Compton-Burnett herself, in a later interview, spoke of her fondness for the theater and for reading plays, particularly Chekhov's, adding,

"I think I should call my books something between a novel and a play, and I feel the form suits me better than the pure play." In their almost total reliance on dialogue, these novels—and particularly the later novels—read like scenarios, and like scenarios they seem to demand the contribution of the theater to enhance their values. But dialogue here is made to bear a greater burden than in either the drama or the conventional novel. It has usurped almost completely the functions of exposition, narrative, and description. And this is possible only because Miss Compton-Burnett's characters are forced to be aware of themselves as both actors in and spectators of the drama. One of their functions is to comment on the action, revealing its implications at any given point. When Fulbert Sullivan (*Parents and Children*), about to leave on a six months' trip to South America, displays some of Lear's paternal egotism by staging an interminable farewell scene, his son Graham remarks: "We have stood and striven faithfully . . . , we have jested with set lips; two of us have wept. Have we not earned our release?" Moreover, these self-conscious characters have a way of viewing themselves in an altogether detached manner, examining their motives publicly, and commenting at one remove on their own behavior. "I must keep my simple ways," says Dudley Gaveston (*A Family and a Fortune*), who has just inherited a modest fortune. "I must not let myself become different. That sounds as if I have admired myself." Or Charity Marcon (*Daughters and Sons*) recounts her day in the British Museum reading room: "I moved about it, a grotesque but dignified figure. Many people looked up to wonder who the tall, strange woman was." In the light of this convention, it is beside the mark to complain that Miss Compton-Burnett's children are unduly precocious and articulate. It is their creator's view of their condition combined with their own deeply felt but unformulated view that they express, rather than the one which by adult consent belongs naturally to their years. "People would hardly believe the pathetic little figure I used to be," says Reuben Donne, age thirteen, referring to his lameness. The observation is detached and artificial without being ironic; dramatically, it is entirely appropriate, for self-pity is not an element of the child's personality.

The point is that Miss Compton-Burnett's characters are never allowed to forget—and never allow us to forget—that they are playing a role. The role may alter from crisis to crisis, but the players are always onstage and they will pause at intervals to review their performance. "So I am to be a hero," remarks Dudley Gaveston. "Well, it will suit me better than it would most people." Or Ellen Mowbray, in *A Father and His Fate:* "I feel I am watching the scene. But I must begin to take my part." Or Cassius Clare (*The Present and the Past*), following a domestic confrontation: "It was an exacting occasion, but I think I arose to it. I think I steered everyone through." Moreover, as in a play these characters have no solitary moments; they are not allowed the consolation of nursing their grief or shame or even, on rare occasions, their happiness in private. Clement Gaveston (*A Family and a Fortune*) laments the fact that his mother can never be alone: "We all live in a chattering crowd, each of us waiting for a chance to be heard." Even their asides, their whispered comments at the dinner table, are overheard. Roderick Shelley (*Two Worlds and Their Ways*) cuts short a private conversation with his wife with the warning "People are about everywhere. Houses hear and see." When the dreadful secrets come to light it is in the full glare of publicity, with the family assembled, and frequently the neighbors, and with the butler listening at the door. Given these circumstances, it strikes one irresistibly that what Miss Compton-Burnett achieved—the essence of her method, in effect—was to raise the art of general conversation, so highly developed in

[21]

England, to the plane of drama. Those family colloquies, which invariably begin with some general discussion of religion or morality or human nature and end with some terrible revelation, are the sole dramatic means. Nothing happens in Miss Compton-Burnett's world that cannot be distilled into conversation and rolled around on the tongue.

The willingness to dispense with verisimilitude gave Miss Compton-Burnett another advantage over both the dramatist and the conventional novelist. It is customary by now to point out that in these novels the discrepancy between appearance and reality—between what the character thinks and what he says, between what he is and what he professes to be—which poses such a problem of representation in drama and in any fictional method of telling a story that strives for objectivity, is in large part eliminated. This is, as we have seen in connection with *Pastors and Masters*, a precarious generalization and one that needs to be qualified. But it is true that to an extraordinary degree these characters, while observing the amenities, say what they think, put aside the mask, so that appearance and reality seem to be one. Nevertheless, the world of masks and appearances—the conventional picture of reality that governs so much of our social behavior—is held constantly in view through the manipulation of clichés. "A poor thing but our own," remarks Susan Marlowe (*Parents and Children*) of the family cottage. "I quite agree with you, my dear," her sister replies. "But why put it in the form of a saying? They don't contain the truth." Just so. But Miss Compton-Burnett does not let the matter rest there. Clichés may not contain the truth but, as a third character adds, "they call attention to it." So in these novels the constant production of saws, maxims, and proverbs of dubious validity enforces a sharp contrast between conventional illusion and the reality of the world as the novelist sees it.

[22]

Miss Compton-Burnett's next novel, *Men and Wives* (1931), consolidates the gains made in *Brothers and Sisters*. It is one of the most ambitious and powerful of her novels, and it exhibits a firmer mastery of structure than its predecessor, though its effort to encompass the full range of village life, somewhat in the *Middlemarch* manner, is one that Miss Compton-Burnett gradually relinquished. Like *Brother and Sisters* a study of the nature and abuses of power, it differs both in the greater depth and subtlety of its psychology and in its management of the conflict, for in this instance the deck is not so clearly stacked, the opponents are more equally matched.

The time is 1889, the scene the country estate of Sir Godfrey Haslam, fifty-six, a good-natured, ineffectual man, the titular head of a family consisting of his neurasthenic wife, Harriet, and four grown children, three boys and a girl. It is Harriet who dominates the family, manages the finances, attempts to guide her children into careers she has chosen for them but for which they have no talents or inclination. Her health is the particular, fussy concern of Godfrey, who is clearly baffled by his strange and recalcitrant brood. The main contest of wills is between Harriet and her oldest son, Matthew, who wants to do medical research though his mother is urging him to establish a practice in London.

Frustrated in her efforts to reform her children, Harriet has become querulous, demanding, a source of constant friction. She spends sleepless nights and tormented days. Following a breakfast quarrel with Matthew, who has taken on himself the burden of opposition that the children feel their weak-willed father should assume, she visits the local doctor and persuades him to give her something that will end her life if she cannot curb her demon. She is, to do her justice, a reluctant tyrant, pathetically aware that she is destroying the family she loves.

[23]

At dinner that evening she defends suicide, and the onslaught of madness is superbly foreshadowed by her secret smiles, her "dreamy tone," and the sudden fits of uncontrollable laughter. It is Matthew who brings on the catastrophe. In spite of Harriet's disapproval he is infatuated with Camilla Bellamy, wife of the local pastor, whose marriage is breaking up. Harriet, excusing herself from the dinner table, comes on her son in the act of opening a letter from Camilla; she voices her displeasure and is cruelly rebuked, whereupon she goes to her room and swallows the tablet the doctor has given her. It proves harmless, as the doctor intended, but the strain induces a breakdown, and Harriet is removed to a hospital.

Six months later she returns home, apparently restored. The family in the interval has learned how to get along without her. Though privately she chafes at her demotion, she is determined to pursue a course of gentle compliance. Her reformation is short-lived. When she makes a final plea to Matthew not to marry Camilla and he in turn is convinced that ultimately she will have her way in the matter, he poisons her, managing to make the death appear a suicide. Overcome with remorse following her funeral, he reveals his guilt first to Camilla, who breaks off their engagement, and then to his family, who reject his confession, preferring to believe that he has inherited his mother's instability and that, repenting his treatment of her, he is the victim of a temporary delusion. This rather blatant dramatic irony carries through the denouement. Harriet, in death, has her way after all: her children leave home to follow the careers she had urged on them from the beginning. Her husband, deprived of her legacy to him if he remarries, is left alone in the house. The last word belongs to one of the family friends: "Harriet was always a fortunate woman."

As in *Brothers and Sisters*, the private tragedy has been enacted in full view of friends, neighbors, and servants, even with their full cooperation. There are no family secrets. Harriet's attempted suicide and Matthew's confession are immediate public property. The curiosity of the villagers is voracious; through some highly developed instinct for disaster they are on the doorstep before the corpse is cold to make their own inquest under the guise of condolence. While Harriet is in the hospital they occupy her house, feed at her table, and ply their host for intelligence. When she returns they are on hand to greet her. From first to last, the characters in Miss Compton-Burnett's novels, victims as well as criminals, must submit to being stripped, exposed, and placed in the dock—only Anna Donne, in *Elders and Betters*, escapes this fate. And as predictable as their unmasking is the way they meet their altered situation, with an aplomb normally reserved for minor discomfitures and a resiliency worthy of a Falstaff. In part a reflection of their monstrous egoism, their behavior has its meaning on a more abstract level. The worst that can be said about human nature, it seems to imply, is after all not so very surprising; the blow is quickly absorbed and everyone accommodates himself, without apparent strain, to the new and diminished view of himself, his world, and his fellow creatures. In conversation the issues posed by conventional morality are endlessly debated, but in action and deed Miss Compton-Burnett's world presents itself as simply amoral. Its single motive is self-interest. Altruism, like that of Dudley Gaveston in *A Family and a Fortune*, may be admired but it is not successful, for it is contrary to human nature. There is in fact a good deal of talk about human nature, as there is about power, in these novels, and none of it is complimentary.

Whether Miss Compton-Burnett's own tolerance of human nature is a direct product of her quasi-deterministic persuasion is not clear. She admitted that she saw all her characters as "in the grip of forces—economic and psychological and hereditary," only to add: "But I suppose that part of people's equipment is a certain power of choice and a strength of will." Which leaves us, if we would try to reconcile these statements, with Original Sin: we have the power to choose but, since corrupted human nature predisposes us to the selfish course, not the power to choose our choices. One thinks of Miss Compton-Burnett's contemporary, Theodore Dreiser, a novelist as remote in spirit and method from her as can be imagined, whose amoral fictional universe provided a kind of refuge, as it did for most American determinists, from the questions that tormented him, who complained that if good was rewarded on this earth, it was not all the good he saw, and that if injustice was punished, it was not all the injustice. Dreiser worried such questions, and to no avail; Miss Compton-Burnett regarded the answers as self-evident. "I don't think guilty people meet punishment in life," she remarked serenely. "I think that the evidence tends to show that crime on the whole pays." When a *New Statesman* reviewer called for a more vindictive ending to *Elders and Betters*, she observed that the journal "wanted wickedness to be punished, but my point is that it is not punished, and that is why it is natural to be guilty of it." And so she could insist that her monsters, like Mathilda Seaton and Josephine Napier, "don't seem to me such monsters as they do to other people," and could add without apparent guile that she felt affection for nearly all of her characters, "for the bad as well as the good." Louise Bogan ascribes much of the power of the novels to the ambiguity of Miss Compton-Burnett's double vision—the comic spirit informing the primarily tragic materials. "Each of them is a nightmare into which we are drawn by degrees but from which we escape with reluctance," she remarks. "For these are high-comedy nightmares." The equanimity with which Miss Compton-Burnett confronts a variety of human aberrations and crimes may be disconcerting, but it is indispensable to the comedy, for the character who engages or repels our feelings too

[26]

strongly is fatal to the comic spirit. In certain of the novels written in the thirties and early forties Miss Compton-Burnett admittedly took risks that endangered the comedy: Harriet Haslam is too sympathetic, Anna Donne and Josephine Napier too hateful. She struck a finer balance in her later novels, but with a corresponding loss of energy and conviction. The extreme detachment of her last novels is not simply a matter of greater refinement of means, or the loss of vitality, but of an acceptance of human foible that is almost Olympian.

More Men Than Women (1933) is a less ambitious novel than its immediate predecessors, more narrowly brilliant, more perverse, and if anything more ruthless in its implications. The roster of crimes is lengthening: in *Brothers and Sisters*, incest; in *Men and Wives*, matricide; in the present novel, murder. The protagonist, Josephine Napier, owner and headmistress of "a large girls' school in a prosperous English town" somewhere near the turn of the century, is one of the most deformed embodiments of human nature in the whole range of Miss Compton-Burnett's exhibit. She is a consummate hypocrite, who manages to conceal her most selfish motives in the garb of altruism. She can lie, connive, and murder with equal ease and equal success, and at the end be eulogized by her closest relative as "a noble creature." As in *Pastors and Masters*, the setting is a school instead of a country house, but the atmosphere is no less claustrophobic. The large family which figures in all but two of the novels is also absent—though with Josephine, the junior and senior mistresses, Josephine's superfluous husband, Simon, and her nephew, Gabriel Swift, all living under the same roof, a kind of ghastly domesticity is achieved. Only the victimized children are missing.

In her will to power and her perverse sexuality, Josephine Napier has one object, to dominate her nephew Gabriel whom she has raised from infancy. He is the son of her widowed brother, Jonathan Swift, a dilettantish writer who for two decades has lived with a former pupil, Felix Bacon, in one of those homosexual arrangements that Miss Compton-Burnett treats in such an oblique and essentially comic way (Felix, fortyish, is introduced sitting on his seventy-year-old mentor's knee). Josephine has sent her nephew through Oxford; now that his education is finished she hopes to keep him around to comfort her old age. Her plan is ultimately frustrated, but not before she has murdered Gabriel's wife. Blackmailed by a member of her staff, she bows to necessity and makes the blackmailer a partner in the school. And although ordinary justice might demand that the will to power defeat its own ends, Josephine conveniently discovers in her accomplice a new outlet for her battered libido.

The structure of the closed society in the last three novels has been matriarchal. In *A House and Its Head* (1935) we have the first major appearance of the father as tyrannus rex: Duncan Edgeworth, "young for his sixty-six years," cold, withdrawn, but imperious and demanding, whose meaner acts—burning books, ordering his sick wife to leave her bed to join the family at breakfast, dropping a prayerbook for his nephew to retrieve—are the daily means by which he sustains his authority. Troubled by his merely human propensities, demanding on himself as well as others, strongly sexed but unable to love, he is a study in exhausted puritanism, for he seeks his salvation in a rigorous adherence to duty and the efficacy of the individual will as a substitute for the love of God. He has two daughters and an orphaned nephew, Grant Edgeworth, whom he both accepts and resents in lieu of a son and heir of his own. When his first wife dies he remarries. The second Mrs. Edgeworth is less than half his age; the marriage proves to be anything but happy; but Alison, the new wife, gives Duncan the son he has longed for and who will deprive his nephew Grant of his inheritance. Not unexpectedly, the child is soon revealed to be Grant's, and there follows one of those scenes of sudden and passionate feeling in which Miss Compton-Burnett excels. When Grant tries to extenuate his behavior as "common to men," Duncan in a fury strikes his nephew in the face. "Grant received it," comments the author, in a superb example of psychological annotation, "in simple relief that the climax had come and passed." Alison in the meantime has fled with another man.

Acting on the bleak assumption that he has no life elsewhere, Grant Edgeworth marries his cousin Sybil. Almost simultaneously Duncan has taken on a third wife in the person of the family governess. Suddenly tragedy strikes the household: Alison's baby is found dead, the gas outlets in his nursery turned on, the windows closed. Suspicion falls on the third wife, now pregnant, and on Duncan, who presumably wants to clear the way for a legitimate heir. But the criminal proves to be the younger daughter, Sybil, who to secure Grant's interest has hired a former Edgeworth family nurse, dismissed from her post, to murder the child. When the truth emerges, Grant leaves Sybil. She goes to live with her invalid Aunt Maria, whom she cultivates so devotedly that the old lady changes her will, leaving everything to her niece. Sybil then uses the legacy to blackmail herself back into the family: she will restore the heirs' original portions provided she can resume her position as Grant's wife and Duncan's affectionate daughter. As in *Men and Wives*, we have as a final ironic tableau one of those family reunions with everyone forced to contemplate a future of living together under the shadow of each other's crimes.

Temporarily, in her next three novels, Miss Compton-Burnett will forsake the more lurid transgressions. There are plenty of nasty characters waiting in the wings, but they will exhibit a more familiar and domestic kind of nastiness. Her next novel, in fact, is more purely comic and only slightly less genial than *Bullivant and the Lambs. Daughters and Sons* (1937) manages a larger cast of hypocrites than any other novel and presents a mother-and-daughter brace of tyrants, but its main thematic concern is a mild one: the inutility of self-sacrifice—which, as Miss Compton-Burnett views it, is merely the other face of power and another form of self-delusion and hypocrisy.

Sabine Ponsonby, an eighty-four-year-old matriarch, and her daughter, Hetta, middle-aged and single, dominate the household of widowed John Ponsonby, a successful but fading popular novelist. The rest of the household consists of five children who collectively pursue a vigorous internecine warfare with Sabine (who hisses at them when she is displeased). One of the older girls, France, has secret literary ambitions; she has written a novel. At a church entertainment, excerpts from the novel are successfully presented in dramatic form. When France is revealed as the author, her father feels a natural jealousy which he is at pains to conceal.

A new governess, Edith Hallam, arrives to replace the most recent one, driven away by Sabine's asperities. Forthright, independent, she makes her way easily with the Ponsonbys, old and young, because she is like them. France, knowing the desperate state of the family finances and anxious to protect her father's ego, arranges with Miss Hallam to use her name in submitting her novel to a publisher. It wins a two-thousand-pound award, and shortly thereafter a check arrives for John Ponsonby, supposedly a gift from an unknown admirer. Sabine, who is given to opening the family mail, discovers Miss Hallam's correspondence with the publisher, learns that it is she who has masqueraded as the unknown admirer, and tells her son, who, touchingly grateful to the governess, proposes and is accepted. Hetta, who since the death of her first sister-in-law has managed her brother's life, nourishing under the guise of sisterly devotion the most appalling self-interest, resorts to a stratagem that several subsequent Compton-Burnett characters will adopt: she disappears leaving a note indicating suicide, then when the family are in a properly contrite mood reappears to enjoy her triumph. The device misfires; the reaction against her is overwhelming; even her doting mother's faith in her is shaken, and the old lady has a stroke. At a dinner party, to which the Ponsonbys have invited their friends, Hetta, now displaced and careless of appearances, denounces her brother in a terrible scene, reveals that France was the "unknown admirer," and concludes her tirade with "What a welter of deceit I have found in my family." Sabine is the only casualty of this passionate encounter; she dies at the table from the shock. And when Hetta finds her destiny in the frail arms of Dr. Chaucer, the local clergyman, who has already made two unsuccessful proposals to the family governesses, Edith Hallam is finally mistress of her own house.

We are back in the moral climate of *Dolores*, but with a difference. The self-serving dedication of a Hetta is the obverse of the "unreasoning service" of a Dolores, though in both cases sacrifice recoils on the agent, who reaps a barren harvest. "The tragedy," observes France, after Hetta has been supplanted by Miss Hallam, "is giving up your life to someone who will not repay you with his own." In the present fable any residual sentiment about the value of sacrifice and suffering is liquidated, not only through the spectacle of Hetta's self-destructive actions, but through the comments of her many victims. When the youngest Ponsonby child asks why Aunt Hetta has been "getting so much worse," she is told that it is because "she tried to live for others." Suffering, it is agreed, is not "wholesome," or as one character remarks, "I have never known anyone improved by it."

The thematic emphasis of *Daughters and Sons* is carried forward into the next novel, *A Family and a Fortune* (1939), with Dudley Gaveston assuming the Dolores role. Unlike Hetta Ponsonby, he is all heart and no head. A bachelor, he lives with his brother Edgar and the latter's family in the paternal mansion. Between the brothers exists a bond deeper than that between Edgar and his wife or children. Edgar's wife, Blanche, is a selfless, lonely, rather pale-tempered soul whose health is in some obscure way threatened. The family, it hardly need be added, is in financial straits. Unexpectedly, Dudley inherits two thousand pounds a year from his godfather. The Gavestons debate how to spend the money, and Dudley, generous by nature and grateful for his small place in the family circle, is happy to share the legacy. But when he falls in love and becomes engaged, the family's new-found security is threatened. Blanche Gaveston's health suddenly worsens, and with that generous regard for the exigencies of the plot that Miss Compton-Burnett's characters exhibit, she dies. This permits Edgar to take advantage of his brother's absence on a business trip to steal his fiancée. Dudley is badly shocked by the betrayal—it is apparent that in one stroke Edgar proposes to alleviate his loneliness and to keep his brother's money in the family—but he goes through the ordeal of the wedding. When he tries to revive the old intimacy with his brother and is rebuffed, he denounces Edgar, quits the house on a winter night, nearly dies of exposure, but survives to reap the full measure of humiliation. In the end he must return, strangely broken and subdued, to resume his minor role in the family scheme. His fate is symptomatic. The good people die or are intimidated; the bad, being tougher and more resilient, survive within the fortress of their egos. In most of the novels the future seems assured only for those who least deserve it.

A Family and a Fortune, says Charles Burkhart, "is all about money." There *is* a good deal of talk about money in the novel; it is as pervasive as the talk about self-sacrifice in *Daughters and Sons*. But Dudley Gaveston's legacy does not corrupt honest men; it merely precipitates the dishonesty, meanness, and treachery latent in certain characters, and is a device to reveal character rather than determine it. Miss Compton-Burnett's characters, as she herself admitted, are static, and her plots, which serve as a developing illustration of character, are usually resolved by a return to the status quo. Her people do not grow; they merely emerge; consequently, it can be argued that the incidents of her plots are merely occasions—elements in a framework, as Kingsley Amis complains, rather than links in a causative sequence involving some kind of change. In fact, as we have noted before, the more violent and unexpected the occasion, the more effective it will be in displacing the mask, vanquishing the illusion, and thrusting the characters into a radical and precarious new relationship. Below the flux they preserve their original identities, but we have come to know them as they are.

For over a decade Miss Compton-Burnett had been producing a novel at regular two-year intervals. ("I'm a biennial," she once remarked.) World War II neither broke her stride nor made its way, even by implication, into her self-contained fictional world. *Parents and Children* (1941) is, on its most coherent level, a study of another of those emotionally alienated, helpless, but generally sympathetic women, like Harriet Haslam, Blanche Gaveston, Jessica Calderon (*Elders and Betters*), and Charlotte Lamb (*Bullivant and the Lambs*), who have no faith in themselves as wives or mothers. Eleanor Sullivan, mother of nine children, cannot define herself in relation to her world or to any of the roles into which she is cast. Out of economic necessity, she and her family live with her husband's parents. Fulbert Sullivan is quite content in this unmanly dependency, especially since his children prefer him to their mother. When he is called to South America on family business, he asks Ridley Cranmer, a bachelor friend and lawyer, to look

[33]

out for the family in his absence. But the latter abuses his trust. Through a complicated stratagem (involving the usual intercepted letter), he persuades the family that Fulbert has died abroad and then proposes to Eleanor, who, frightened at being alone with the children she does not understand and who do not understand her, accepts him. On the day before the wedding Fulbert makes an Enoch-Arden-like return, unmasks the false friend, and reclaims his wife. No such bare synopsis will indicate how tightly Miss Compton-Burnett has bound her characters in a circle of guilt. Fulbert is the exception—the only character who comes through morally untarnished—and he is not a sympathetic figure. It is one of those characteristic and depressing ironies that precludes any balancing of accounts in Miss Compton-Burnett's moral universe.

Depending on one's reading of Miss Compton-Burnett, one might call her next novel, *Elders and Betters* (1944), either her most cynical or her most steadfastly undisillusioned. The action moves between the two households of Benjamin Donne and his brother-in-law, Thomas Calderon, both in their sixties. Benjamin has recently moved his family into the Calderon neighborhood in order to be near his sisters, Jessica Calderon, mother of a large family, and Susan, or "Sukey" Donne, an unmarried invalid and the spoiled, autocratic darling of both families. The Calderon children embrace the usual spectrum of age and experience (or inexperience): Julius and Theodora, ages eleven and ten, who, alienated withindoors, escape to the garden to worship their private gods, Chung and his beloved son Chung Li; Terence, in his mid-twenties, who on leaving Oxford has settled at home to do nothing; and Tullia, slightly younger, who is as devoted to her pale neurasthenic mother as Terence is to his father. The family has been made to feel a deep collective guilt because they do not pay enough attention to the invalid Sukey, who over the years has bewailed her heart trouble and her imminent demise until the family's capacity for sustained devotion has been exhausted.

Into this atmosphere come Benjamin Donne and his children: Anna, thirty, the only daughter, a dwarfish woman with a large head—a female Richard III, as it turns out, with a soul as deformed as her body—and three sons, Bernard, "a large stout young man of thirty-two" who is one of Miss Compton-Burnett's "good" people, Esmond, twenty-six, limp, irritable, and at odds with his family, and Reuben, thirteen, lamed, nervous, sad, and very precocious. It is the domineering Anna who arrives first on the scene, chooses a house, settles it, and who immediately sizes up her relatives' situation, discerns her opportunity, and quietly prepares to exploit it. Over the next few weeks she makes herself indispensable to the ailing Sukey. Ultimately the latter, in one of her recurrent fits of pique against her sister, makes a new will favoring Anna—a game she has played for years—and then, regretting the action, instructs Anna to burn the new will. Anna does the opposite: she puts the new one in Sukey's desk and burns the old. Sukey dies, and the Calderons, disinherited, are left only with an aggravated sense of guilt. The mother Jessica, who suspects skulduggery, privately appeals to Anna to make things right and is defeated in a brutal scene in which Anna, probing the vulnerable spot, convinces her aunt that even her family finds her difficult. Jessica commits suicide. Anna, undaunted, sets her cap for Terence Calderon, who would marry anyone rather than work. The novel ends with the youngest Calderons returning to their devotions at the garden altar and cruelly turning away the lamed Reuben Donne. The implication is clear: they have entered the selfish world of adulthood.

In contrast with the other novels, the cold war in *Elders and Betters* is waged with a difference: only Anna and Jessica are aware that there *is* a war, victor and victim are never identified as such, and all of the characters except Anna are casualties. It is a grimmer work even than *Brothers and Sisters*, possibly because the events (the conclusion, with its game of marital musical chairs, excluded) cleave more narrowly to probability. At one point in the novel one can imagine Miss Compton-Burnett conducting a dialogue with herself through the medium of two of her characters. When Tullia Calderon observes, "Things are better, brought into the light of day," and her brother Terence replies, "Would you sap the very foundations of civilization?" the novelist defines the terms of an impossible equation and one which is at the very heart of the larger dialogue conducted in her fiction as a whole. Do we survive, individually and as a society, by virtue of our illusions? An affirmative answer is somehow implicit in the comic view of life, just as the tragic view suggests that illusion must be vanquished before order can be restored—that ripeness is all. And in Miss Compton-Burnett's fiction both views remain active and unresolved. "Things only ferment and fester in the dark," remarks a character in *Bullivant and the Lambs*. "It is the hidden thing that cannot flourish," declares Sir Roderick Shelley, in *Two Worlds and Their Ways*. "Nothing can grow without the light." But when the light is shed, its effect is to stunt growth; it is more than most of Miss Compton-Burnett's children of the dark can bear. They are left with only the sad knowledge that the remainder of their lives is somehow diminished. The crisis of illumination deprives them of the old power to feel deeply or protest their fate. "Yes, well, I must pick myself up," says Godfrey Haslam, in weary self-admonition, after the family tragedy has run its course. "I have a good deal of life before me. I must not let myself sink to the level of bitterness." When the crisis has passed, the walls begin to close in. To Nance Edgeworth's "What incredible things happen in this house," her brother Grant can only reply, "Nothing can happen to us outside it. We have no life elsewhere." Once the secret is out, the guilt acknowledged, and the passion spent, the old order reasserts itself. It will survive until the next generation revives the cycle, as it assuredly will, and reenacts the whole drama of temptation, fall, repentance, and expiation.

Bullivant and the Lambs (1947), which reintroduced Miss Compton-Burnett to American readers after a long period of neglect, is by general consent her most satisfying performance (though it is not easy to establish priorities in a canon that exhibits such internal consistency and such lack of experiment or development). Its structure is simpler and firmer than that of most of her novels; its tone, striving as always to mediate between the comic and the macabre, achieves a kind of equilibrium not always apparent in her work; and her major characters —the domestic martinet Horace Lamb, his dependent cousin Mortimer Lamb, and the memorable Bullivant—not only are vivid in outline but they interact at great depth and with a profound complexity of motive. Superficially, it is also the most Dickensian of her novels. Horace Lamb is in the Murdstone tradition—severe in his demands, niggardly with his stores —and his children, dressed in hand-me-downs, underfed, pale and chattering with cold, and frightened of their father, are Dickensian waifs. There is also Miss Buchanan, whom Dickens would have admired, who runs a village shop and with marvelous resourcefulness guards the pitiful secret that she cannot read or write. In no previous novel, moreover, has Miss Compton-Burnett explored the life belowstairs with such thoroughness and obvious delight. The butler, Bullivant, is as much a sovereign in his demesne as Horace is in his, and toward his inferiors he manifests the same air of paternal skepticism and disapproval that marks Horace Lamb's dealings with his children. With his betters, on the other hand, he is the perfect servant, loyal, discreet (he has, he asserts, "the knowledge of what to know, and what not know"), deferential, and efficient. He has served in the house for forty-five years. "A servant I am, and a servant I remain," he intones. "So it is; so it has been; so it will be; and I am satisfied."

As for Horace Lamb, it is difficult to know how much compassion, if indeed any, he is supposed to elicit. He is irritable, self-righteous, and forever prying, but he is also uncertain of himself, of his family's love for him, and therefore lonely, with the result that he makes life harsh and unbearable for everyone around him. He has married for money, as his wife, Charlotte, has married for love, and both have been disappointed. He suffers constant blows to his self-esteem. His wife is in love with his cousin Mortimer, his children guiltily wish his death (one of them molds a tallow image of his father, sticks pins into it, and is gratified to hear that Horace has had a sudden attack of rheumatism), and his footman tries to murder him. When he relaxes his despotism, the family lives in perpetual fear that his old self will return. Exhausted by his fluctuating moods of outrage, recrimination, and forced benevolence, he falls dangerously ill. Summoning the family to his sickroom, he stages an interminable deathbed scene in which he asks their forgiveness. But since it is part of the comedy that the heroic gestures of Miss Compton-Burnett's characters are always being spoiled by the vagaries of fate, he unexpectedly recovers and then finds it necessary to maintain the character he has assumed on his imaginary deathbed. In the meantime resistance to his tyranny has ended with the family's recognition that the mold into which their lives have been cast has hardened, and the novel ends as it began, with Horace complaining to Bullivant of a smoking fire and an obstruction in the chimney.

Even Miss Compton-Burnett's most loyal admirers may feel that after *Bullivant and the Lambs* her powers began to diminish and that she tended to repeat her successes, particularly with certain types of characters and situations. There are gains as well as losses: her children become increasingly more attractive as her butlers decline in stature and interest, and there is a certain pleasure, mainly aesthetic, in watching the novelist gradually refine her method, paring her means to a minimum, until by the time she writes *A God and His Gifts* (1963) the presentation is as abstract as the form can conceivably bear. But beginning in the fifties one has the nagging feeling that the novels, still emerging at regular two-year intervals, are in large part products of will and a habit of self-discipline perfected over the years. This may simply be an unfortunate way of generalizing from the feeling that the earlier novels are as a group more deeply felt, more original, and more forcible in their impact than the later novels, and it may do less than justice to the fact that Miss Compton-Burnett continued to exert her peculiar charm in a way that put most of her contemporaries at a disadvantage.

Nevertheless, there are certain tendencies in the later novels which are already apparent in her next novel, *Two Worlds and Their Ways* (1949). The plot, which has been admired because it balances off the exposure of the children's misdeeds in school against the subsequent revelation of their elders' foibles and crimes, is merely neat and somewhat mechanical; and the invention in the last chapters, with the gratuitous pother over a lost earring, is both elaborate and tedious. One is aware too of Miss Compton-Burnett's growing habit of attenuating her episodes until the talk becomes tiresome as the topic is relentlessly fletcherized. And finally, given her many characters and her casual way of establishing their identities, is it fair to confront even the devoted reader with two Maria Shelleys, both wives of the same man, and three closely related Olivers (Firebrace, Shelley, and Spode)? There is much to recommend the novel —the episodes of school life are brilliantly handled, and the children themselves are appealing—but it is a matter of diminishing returns as the plot, in its later convoluted development, slowly strangles both the wit and the fable.

It is the more dismaying, consequently, to find that the novel that follows it, *Darkness and Day* (1951), is perhaps the weakest of Miss Compton-Burnett's works. It is also her most somber. In no other novel are the characters so isolated, from the world, from those closest to them, and even from themselves, or so obsessed with thoughts of mutability, lost opportunities, and death. Edmund and Bridget Lovat move in their own peculiar darkness, for they have reason to believe that though husband and wife they are also father and daughter. Bridget is consequently the extreme development of that familiar type in the novels, the guilt-ridden matron who is oppressive to her family because she is oppressive to herself. The Lovat children, two small daughters who have lived under the burden of an undefined threat, are predictably harder and more self-contained than most of Miss Compton-Burnett's children—a Goneril and Regan in miniature—and the scene in which they bait their governess, who at first fights back and then is gradually driven from the field, is one of the finest in all the novels. But generally one senses a weariness of spirit in these pages, and the burden of a story potentially tragic but which will not shape itself to the proper dimensions. The style is terser than usual but also more elliptical, and there are longueurs that are hard to forgive, principally the tedious sessions of servant talk in which Miss Compton-Burnett may have been trying, inadvisedly, to repeat her success in *Bullivant and the Lambs*.

The Present and the Past (1953) has a plot so natural as to make it seem a sport. There are no intercepted letters or stolen wills, and the overheard conversations do not function crucially in the development. Again, as in all the novels after *A Family and a Fortune*, the setting is limited to two houses and the cast

[40]

to their occupants—the host of prying villagers having long since disappeared, bequeathing their function to the belowstairs gossips. The basic cast has in fact become rather stabilized: Father, either too detached or too demanding; Mother, neurotically unsure of herself, loving her children but unable to protect them; the children, averaging about five in number; the descending hierarchy of tutors, governesses, nurses, butler, cook, and adolescent menials; and the occupants of the Other House, usually an unmarried brother-sister combination—sometimes with an aged parent, sometimes not—who live a tidy, unthreatened, unambitious cottage life.

We have met Cassius Clare before, in various guises. He is the self-centered husband and father, the household despot, who requires more sympathy and reassurance than his family can provide. Twice married, he has fathered two sets of children, but he is closest perhaps to his father and to the butler, Ainger, who serves him devotedly and fends off inquiries from the kitchen gossips. When Cassius's first wife, Catherine Scrope, suddenly reappears in the neighborhood, his vanity is understandably whetted by the prospect of a meeting between her and his present wife, Flavia. But when they strike up a close friendship and he is left increasingly to himself, he fakes a suicide to regain the center of attention. The device miscarries, and he is exposed. Characteristically, he is too egocentric to be abashed. Nevertheless, when it grows on him that he has lost the respect of his family, he frets, becomes depressed, and finally makes a second, this time successful, attempt on his life. Flavia and Catherine, in a penitential mood, relinquish their friendship, and the latter, before quitting the neighborhood forever, forces her children by Cassius to choose between herself and their adopted mother. The family's postmortem verdict on Cassius—that he was a better man than he showed himself—is so tolerant that we must regard it as an expression not so much of the characters' experience as of the novelist's superior detachment.

Like *More Men Than Women*, Miss Compton-Burnett's next novel, *Mother and Son* (1955), is preoccupied with the distaff side. Its dominating characters are women, and its action is divided between the household of Miss Emma Greatheart, who lives with two spinster servant-companions, Miss Burke and Miss Wolsey, and that of the Hume family, where the foreground of the domestic picture is occupied by the savagely matriarchal Miranda and her docile, womanish son, Rosebery. Julius Hume, twelve years younger than his wife, and his two young nephews and a niece—orphans whose expectations are even dimmer than those of most of Miss Compton-Burnett's children—complete the family group. The destinies of the two households are conjoined when Hester Wolsey, who has been fretting in her dependence, is engaged by Miranda as a companion.

When Miranda tells her husband that she is gravely ill and may die, he confesses that the nephews and niece are his illegitimate children. Miranda is harshly forgiving, but the revelation hastens her death. Rosebery, going through his mother's papers, discovers that Julius is not his father and that he too is illegitimate. Deprived at a stroke of both parents, the Rosebery who has been unable to defy his mother, even to the extent of drinking his tea without sugar, now exhibits a kind of pathetic manliness. He gives up his claim to Julius's money in favor of the latter's illegitimate children, and on the rebound from the loss of his mother proposes to Miss Wolsey. The latter, with her eye on bigger game, refuses him because she is confident that she has made herself indispensable to the widowed Julius. Her strategy miscarries when Julius persuades Miss Greatheart to marry him and the rejected Rosebery becomes engaged to Miss Burke. Hester, who by now is in possession of the family secrets, gets her revenge by telling all. The engagements are broken, the spinsters reunited under Emma Greatheart's roof, and Rosebery, after giving up his scheme to travel the world in search of his real father, decides to remain as a guest in the only home he has ever known. Again, as in all the novels before *Mother and Son*, everything has changed and nothing has changed.

Among Miss Compton-Burnett's last four novels, only *A God and His Gifts* (1963) moves somewhat beyond the established mode. The three that precede it, *A Father and His Fate* (1957), *A Heritage and Its History* (1959), and *The Mighty and Their Fall* (1961), rework the formula with only one or two minor innovations. All four novels feature the self-regarding male who asserts his own claims to the detriment of his family; all make use of incest, threatened if not actual. *The Mighty and Their Fall* contains in their purest form practically all the classic ingredients of the Compton-Burnett novel, such as the exchanged wills, the intercepted letter, the overheard conversation. *A Father and His Fate* employs two less overworked but equally familiar devices to get the plot moving: the hoax perpetrated by the tyrant to exact emotional tribute from his family, and the Enoch Arden motif of shipwreck and unexpected return. All the novels except *A God and His Gifts* testify again to Miss Compton-Burnett's interest in the character of the elderly man, usually a widower, who marries a much younger woman and by introducing a stranger into the household subverts the memory of the mother and the authority of the eldest daughter. If there is anything unexpected in the novelist's later manner it is, first of all, her attempt in two of the novels, *A Heritage and Its History* and *A God and His Gifts*, to extend her time scheme to embrace several generations of family history, and, second, the appearance of a new type of female character (Verena Gray in *A Father and His Fate* and Teresa Chilton in *The Mighty and*

Their Fall), almost Brontë-like in its suggestions of strange, intense, and willful passions. All one can finally say of these last novels as a group is that we are moving deeper into a claustrophobic world in which the contest for money or power is waged entirely within the walls of what Edward Sackville-West has called "these embowered, rook-enchanted concentration camps" and without the distractions which in the earlier novels arose from the claims or opinions of outsiders.

For the admirers of Miss Compton-Burnett's work who for a decade had kept the faith with mounting if affectionate dismay, her last novel must have appeared as an unexpected bonus. As an introduction to her work, *A God and His Gifts* would hardly do, for it represents the novelist and her method at their most eccentric pitch. But it is a novel of great interest, if only because for the first time in her fiction there is an explicit mythic element. Hereward Egerton, the novelist-protagonist, who leaves his mistress, takes a wife, betrays her with her sister, and then, dropping down a generation, exercises a kind of *droit du seigneur* over his sons' wives and fiancées, is a rampant fertility god; and his family, which comes to include his illegitimate children by a daughter-in-law and a sister-in-law, is like some Adam-race sprung from the loins of a single progenitor. Egerton is human as the gods of mythology are human. His failings derive from his strength and are inseparable from it. He is a man, in his own words, "of great powers, swift passions and a generous heart," and his family not only suffers greatly but benefits greatly from these traits. The "gifts" of the title are threefold: they are in one sense his talent, in another the gifts—of heart and mind as well as purse—he has bestowed, in still another the gifts he has received, mainly in the form of compliance from many women. It is a remarkable tour de force characterization. Hereward Egerton is the tyrant seen in a new light, as a natural force which in its wayward expression dooms four generations of a family to comic futility. In no other novel, moreover, did Miss Compton-Burnett have so much to say about the nature of the artist, his consuming and necessary egoism, and the godlike aspect of the creative spirit. And although nothing she has to say on the subject seems very new, what is remarkable is how the stereotype is forced to give way under the pressure of Hereward Egerton's complex human qualities. Her last major character is her most human, and he speaks from an experience that seems to reflect the novelist's own attitudes toward her art and the materials of her art. As a valedictory performance, *A God and His Gifts* is both appropriate and deeply moving.

SELECTED BIBLIOGRAPHY

PRINCIPAL WORKS OF IVY COMPTON-BURNETT

Dolores. Edinburgh and London, William Blackwood and Sons, 1911.

Pastors and Masters: A Study. London, Heath Cranton, 1925; London, Victor Gollancz, 1952.

Brothers and Sisters. London, Heath Cranton, 1929; New York, Harcourt, Brace, 1929.

Men and Wives. London, William Heinemann, 1931; New York, Harcourt, Brace, 1931.

More Women Than Men. London, William Heinemann, 1933.

A House and Its Head. London, William Heinemann, 1935.

Daughters and Sons. London, Victor Gollancz, 1937; New York, Norton, 1938.

A Family and a Fortune. London, Victor Gollancz, 1939.

Parents and Children. London, Victor Gollancz, 1941.

Elders and Betters. London, Victor Gollancz, 1944.

Manservant and Maidservant. London, Victor Gollancz, 1947; published in the United States as Bullivant and the Lambs. New York, Alfred A. Knopf, 1947.

Two Worlds and Their Ways. London, Victor Gollancz, 1949; New York, Alfred A. Knopf, 1949.

Darkness and Day. London, Victor Gollancz, 1951; New York, Alfred A. Knopf, 1951.

The Present and the Past. London, Victor Gollancz, 1953; New York, Julian Messner, 1953.

Mother and Son. London, Victor Gollancz, 1955; New York, Julian Messner, 1955.

A Father and His Fate. London, Victor Gollancz, 1957.

A Heritage and Its History. London, Victor Gollancz, 1959; New York, Simon and Schuster, 1959.

The Mighty and Their Fall. London, Victor Gollancz, 1961; New York, Simon and Schuster, 1962.

A God and His Gifts. London, Victor Gollancz, 1963; New York, Simon and Schuster, 1964.

CRITICAL WORKS AND COMMENTARY

Amis, Kingsley. "One World and Its Way" (review of Robert Liddell's The Novels of I. Compton-Burnett), *Twentieth Century*, CLVIII (August, 1950), 168–75.

Baldanza, Frank. Ivy Compton-Burnett. New York, Twayne, 1964.

Bogan, Louise. "Childhood's False Eden: I. Compton-Burnett," in Selected Criticism. New York, Noonday Press, 1955. Pp. 189–90.

Bowen, Elizabeth. "Ivy Compton-Burnett," in Collected Impressions. New York, Alfred A. Knopf, 1950. Pp. 82–91.

Burkhart, Charles. I. Compton-Burnett. London, Victor Gollancz, 1965.

Compton-Burnett, I., and M. Jourdain. "A Conversation," in Orion: A Miscellany, Vol. I. London, Weidenfeld and Nicholson, 1945. Pp. 20–28.

Greenfield, Stanley B. " 'Pastors and Masters': The Spoils of Genius," *Criticism*, II (Winter, 1960), 66–80.

"Interview with Miss Compton-Burnett," *Review of English Literature*, III (October, 1962), 96–112.

Jefferson, D. W. "A Note on Ivy Compton-Burnett," *Review of English Literature*, I (April, 1960), 19–24.

Johnson, Pamela Hansford. I. Compton-Burnett. Supplement to *British Book News*. London, New York, and Toronto, Longmans, Green & Co., 1951.

——— "Three Novelists and the Drawing of Character: C. P. Snow, Joyce Cary and Ivy Compton-Burnett," *Essays and Studies*, N.S., III (1950), 82–99.

Kermode, Frank. "The House of Fiction: Interviews with Seven English Novelists," *Partisan Review*, XXX (Spring, 1963), 61–82.

Liddell, Robert. "The Novels of I. Compton-Burnett." Appendix III in A Treatise on the Novel. London, Jonathan Cape, 1947. Pp. 146–63.

——— The Novels of I. Compton-Burnett. London, Victor Gollancz, 1955.

McCabe, Bernard. "Ivy Compton-Burnett: An English Eccentric," *Critique*, III, No. 2 (1960), 47–63.

McCarthy, Mary. "The Inventions of I. Compton-Burnett," *Encounter*, XXVII (November, 1966), 19–31.

Pritchett, V. S. "Miss Compton-Burnett" (review of Robert Liddell's The Novels of I. Compton-Burnett), *New Statesman and Nation*, N.S., XLIX (March 5, 1955), 328–29.

Sackville-West, Edward. "Ladies Whose Bright Pens . . . ," in Inclinations. New York, Charles Scribner's Sons, 1949. Pp. 78–103.

Strachey, Richard. "The Works of Ivy Compton-Burnett," *Life and Letters*, XII (April, 1935), 30–36.

West, Anthony. "Ivy Compton-Burnett," in Principles and Persuasions. New York, Harcourt, Brace, 1957. Pp. 225–32.

Wilson, Angus. "Ivy Compton-Burnett" (review of Robert Liddell's The Novels of I. Compton-Burnett), *London Magazine*, II (July, 1955), 64–70.